EMILY'S GIFT
THE TRUE STORY OF SHERLOCK & JACKSON

ELLEN SHANE

ART WORK BY:

BERNARD JOAQUIN
PATRICK HORAN

Has someone told you that you can't have something you really, really want?

This story is about a young girl who didn't let that stand in her way.

She would not give up.

ELLEN SHANE   BERNARD JOAQUIN   PATRICK HORAN

The youngest of three sisters, Emily dreamed of owning a dog.

In fact, each of her older sisters always wanted one, too. But while their mom, Mrs. Shane, loved animals, she didn't want the extra work. "Someone has to feed, walk, and clean up after a dog," she said. "Then, there's the cost of the food, vet bills…and who will look after the dog if we go away?"

And then there was Emily's dad, whose terrible allergies made owning a dog impossible. Animals made him sick. So did trees, dust, mold and many other things.

So, the answer to Emily owning a dog was always "no."

Before Emily was born, the family was made up of two girls, their mom and dad. No pets! (At least, not yet!)

The oldest daughter was named Gerri and her younger sister was named Leigh. Long before Emily was born, when Gerri was little, she wanted a pet very badly. So did Leigh.

If Gerri saw a ladybug, she would want to keep it as a pet. Deep down, she truly desired a dog, cat or any animal with fur. But rules are rules. Furry pets were not allowed in their home.

Eventually, Mrs. Shane took the two girls to the pet store in search of a cuddly, family friend to take home. They came home with a new family member - a "skinny pig."

"What's that?" asked Mr. Shane.

"It's a guinea pig with no fur," said Gerri. The man at the pet store said that he wouldn't bother your allergies," she said with a big smile.

"He looks like a lab experiment," said her dad, while gazing up-and-down at the odd-looking creature.

Gerri named their new family pet "Sparky." And, the skinny pig was indeed a furless guinea pig. He had grayish black skin, with a wide band of pink around his middle that looked like a belt. He ate lots of pellet food, made noises and crawled around. The family made Sparky feel right at home. They created a hammock inside his cage with a small towel.

Sparky loved to hide underneath it. Gerri would take him out of the cage, and Sparky would settle in her lap after crawling around on the floor. He often tried to nip people with his teeth – but he never nipped Gerri. Sparky loved eating salad greens. Whenever he heard any type of chopping sound that indicated vegetables were being prepared, Sparky would get excited and make loud noises.

Best of all, Mr. Shane was not allergic to Sparky.

After many years, the Shane family moved to Malibu, California. It was a big change from living in Montreal, Canada. No more cold, snowy winters! Everyone loved the mostly sunny days, the beaches, and living in the mountains.

Emily was born very shortly after the big move to Malibu – on August 9, 1996. Now there were three darling, daughters. By that time, Sparky was quite old. He had lived a full life for a guinea pig. The Shanes no longer had their family pet.

One day, when Emily was 13 years old, she sent her mom a text message.

She wrote, "Can we get a puppy?" Emily was hoping to convince her parents to bring a pet into their home again. "No!" her mom answered. When Emily asked why, her mom did not text back a list. However, Emily knew the reasons. They had been over them many times.

First, there was her dad's allergies. Then, there was all the extra work puppies would bring - cleaning up after them, training them, feeding, walking, bathing, etc.

But Emily didn't give up. Her friend at school had shown Emily photos of his dog's new litter. The puppies looked so adorable and irresistible. Emily wanted one of those puppies more than anything in the world. She sent her mom another text that looked like this:

There on Mrs. Shane's phone was a photo of the cutest, seven-week-old Jack Russell puppy. The puppy's face was exactly half white, and half black-and-brown.

What do you think happened?

Emily's mom looked at the picture and thought to herself, "That is THE cutest puppy!" Mrs. Shane didn't think about extra work, vet bills or walks. She didn't think about messes from accidents.

However, she did think about her husband's allergies. But not for long! She mostly thought, "How adorable! How precious!"

Mrs. Shane texted Emily a reply. "Maybe we'll go and look at him."

The two went to "look" at the cutest puppy ever!

When they arrived at Emily's friend's house, they saw the litter of puppies, including the puppy whose picture Emily texted. He had the cutest face. Each side of his face was a different color - just like the photo. His tail curled up like a little pig's, and his ears flopped.

There was one other puppy in the litter who still needed a home. He had a marking on his head that looked like a check mark.

If you looked closely, it was actually the shape of a heart, with a line on one side like this:

His tail was long and straight. His ears were straight and pointed. The puppies were so tiny and adorable!

They welcomed Emily and her mom with licks, and excitedly ran around before climbing into their arms. Emily and her mom cradled them, looked at their faces, and fell in love. There was no turning back.

The very next day, Emily and Leigh went with their mom to bring the puppies home. The girls walked into their home, cuddling their two new pets. Their dad was rather shocked and surprised! "What are you doing? What is going on?" Mr. Shane asked.

"Look at our two puppies," the girls said together.

"What??? What about my allergies?" Mr. Shane asked.

Mrs. Shane said, "If you get sick or have a bad allergic reaction, somebody will want these adorable puppies. Almost everyone in our neighborhood has dogs. We just had to bring these puppies home. They are so precious."

The puppy in Emily's arms excitedly licked her face as she cradled him. Needless to say, Mr. Shane was not pleased. "I want nothing to do with this. Absolutely nothing!" he declared.

Here's what happened. Mr. Shane did get sick. For ten days, his nose was running, his eyes watered, were red and very itchy. He also coughed a lot.

The girls wondered how long this would continue. Would they really have to give their precious puppies away?

Then, something amazing happened! All of Mr. Shane's allergy symptoms started to go away. Soon, they disappeared altogether. It was like a miracle!

Emily claimed the dog with the half white, half black-and-brown face as hers. She named him "Jackson."

When the other puppy first walked into the house, he immediately began investigating every room, every corner, and every inch of the house.

Gerri said, "Look! He's just like Sherlock Holmes the detective – he's inspecting every inch of the house!" That was it. Leigh claimed that dog as hers and named him "Sherlock."

The puppies slept in a small enclosure in a cozy dog bed. The girls covered it with soft blankets. The puppies would snuggle together and sleep. When they were awake, they would play and scamper around.

The girls would pick them up and play with them. Then, the puppies would curl up on them and fall fast asleep again.

The Shane family no longer needed an alarm to wake up in the morning. The puppies were up before dawn, whimpering and scurrying around. The girls didn't mind, as they wanted time with their pets before leaving for school.

They had never been up and ready so early!

Taking care of Sherlock and Jackson was a huge responsibility. But, the girls were up for the challenge. They fed and cleaned up after the puppies. They spent time training them with their mom.

And of course, they spent many hours playing with them. The puppies brought everyone so much joy.

Emily was so proud that she was the one who brought dogs into the Shane household. She truly couldn't believe it! Her dream came true!

Remember that sometimes a "no" can turn into a "yes!"

Just like Emily, you may feel angry or upset or frustrated because you can't have something you really, really want. It may come to you.

Be patient and always think positive.

Another thing: Mr. Shane ended up loving "the boys" as much as everyone else in the family.

He went from wanting nothing to do with them to playing, walking, and feeding them, too!

The End

Dedication

This book was written in loving memory of Emily Rose Shane, who really did bring Sherlock and Jackson into our lives. Their presence is truly a gift.

My wish is for the Emily Shane Foundation (www.emilyshane.org) to thrive in its mission. This nonprofit charity honors Emily's memory by serving disadvantaged, middle school students across Los Angeles and Ventura counties.

May a dog or other pet bring joy to your life!

--- *Ellen Shane*

Emily with Jackson

About the Author

Ellen Shane is a dog lover, wife, mother, public speaker, and co-founder of The Emily Shane Foundation. The Foundation is a nonprofit charity that honors Emily's memory by empowering disadvantaged middle school students across Los Angeles and Ventura counties with its Successful Educational Achievement (SEA) Program. The students benefiting from the SEA Program are at-risk of academic failure in mainstream classrooms.

The Foundation is dedicated to promoting compassion and empathy by encouraging a "Pass it Forward" mindset. Each SEA Program participant must perform a good deed or act of kindness in return for the support they receive. Please visit www.emilyshane.org for further information.

In addition to Ellen's work with the Foundation, she provides private grief support counseling.

Emily's Gift is the first in a series of books based on true stories of the two dogs who came into the lives of Ellen and her family.

For speaking engagements and author interviews or to invite Ellen Shane to speak, please contact info@emilyshane.org or call 213-290-5441.

Copyright 2020 by Ellen Shane

All rights reserved. In accordance with the U.S. Copyright Act of 1976, the scanning, uploading, and electronic sharing of any part of this book without the permission of the publisher is unlawful piracy ad theft of the author's intellectual property. If you would like to use material from this book (other than for review purposes), prior written permission must be obtained by contacting the publisher at info@knowledgepowerinc.com

Thank you for your support of the author's rights.

ISBN: 978-1-950936-34-2 Hardback
ISBN: 978-1-950936-35-9 Paperback
Library of Congress Control Number: Pending

Editor: Penny Scott
Illustrators: Bernard Joaquin and Patrick Horan

Published by:
KP Publishing
Valencia, CA 91355
www.kp-pub.com

Printed in the United States of America

www.ingramcontent.com/pod-product-compliance
Lightning Source LLC
Chambersburg PA
CBHW042110090526
44592CB00004B/75